LeBron James

The Inspiring Story of NBA Superstar LeBron James

Table of Contents

Introduction

Thank you for taking the time to read this book on LeBron James!

This book covers the topic of NBA superstar, LeBron James. In the following chapters you will learn about LeBron's early life, his high school career, his NBA career to date, his life outside of basketball, and much more.

LeBron is widely regarded as one of the best athletes to have ever lived. As you will soon discover, LeBron has achieved a lot not only on the court, but also outside of basketball. A philanthropist and political activist, LeBron's impact reaches far and wide.

At the completion of this book you will have a good understanding of the life of LeBron James, including his career, his life off of the basketball court, and what is likely to be next for the NBA champion.

Once again, thanks for choosing this book, I hope you enjoy it!

Chapter 1: Who Is LeBron James

Anyone who loves basketball knows LeBron James. He is a professional player that stands 6 feet 8 inches and weighs 250 pounds. He is a living basketball hero and an athlete par excellence. He is hailed by many people as the world's best basketball player, and the greatest NBA player of all time.

This NBA Superstar is a man of versatility. The highlights of his basketball career include one NBA Scoring title, two Olympic Gold Medals, three NBA Finals MVP Awards, three All-Star Game MVP Awards, and four NBA Most Valuable Player Awards.

Early Life

He was born LeBron Raymone James on December 30, 1984, in Akron, Ohio. His mother, Gloria Marie James gave birth to him when she was only 16 and raised him single-handedly. His mom and father, Anthony McClelland, who was an ex-convict with a long history of criminal convictions, were separated.

Life was difficult during his early years. His mom struggled between accounting and retail jobs to pay the bills. They often moved from one apartment to another in search of better employment. Despite their difficult life, Gloria shielded him from violence and poverty. She was a loving mom who indulged his interest in basketball.

When he was in elementary school, Gloria realized that her son needed stability. She wanted to give young LeBron a more stable family environment instead of a nomadic lifestyle. They had a heart-to-heart mother and son talk. Then, she allowed him to live with Frank Walker. Walker was a local football coach who trained youth in the community. At age 9, he introduced James to another ball game - basketball.

LeBron's early idol was Michael Jordan. He patterned his moves after him like launching jumpers and taking it to the hole. When he was in fifth grade, James began playing organized basketball. He became a member of the Northeast Ohio Shooting Stars who competed in the Amateur Athletic Union (AAU). He and team buddies Sian Cotton, Willie McGee, and Dru Joyce III led the team to local and national championships. They dubbed their mighty group as the "Fab Four" and they made a pact to attend high school together.

Their decision to study at St. Vincent-St. Mary High School caused a bit of local controversy because it was a private Catholic school that was predominately white, whereas all members of the Fab-Four were African American.

High School Career

Basketball

When James started playing for St. Vincent-St. Mary High School varsity team, The Fighting Irish, he was touted as a future NBA superstar by the national media. He averaged 21 points and 6 rebounds a game during his freshman year. His team held a 27-0 record which made them Ohio's only boys' high school team that was undefeated at the end of the season, earning them an invitation to the Division III state championship.

In his sophomore year, James was chosen to USA Today's All-USA First Team, and earned the Ohio Mr. Basketball title. He was the first sophomore player to ever achieve this feat! He led the Fighting Irish to a 26-1 record, becoming the state champions for a second time. James averaged 25.2 points, 5.8 assists, 7.2 rebounds, and 3.8 steals per game.

To satisfy the demand of NBA and college scouts, alumni, and fans wanting to see James play, St. Vincent-St. Mary decided to hold their home games at the University of Akron. The school's Rhodes Arena boasted a seating capacity of 5,492.

Before his junior year, he was featured in the SLAM Magazine by writer Ryan Jones. He lauded the young superstar as "America's best high school player in basketball."

James also graced the cover of Sports Illustrated during the season. He was the first ever underclassman to do it.

In his junior year, he averaged 29 points, 5.7 assists, 8.3 rebounds, and 3.3 steals per game. Once again, James became the Ohio Mr. Basketball, and was chosen to be on the USA Today's All-USA First Team. He was also named as the Gatorade National Player of the Year. The high school team finished the year with a 23-4 record, barely missing out on a spot in the Division II finals.

The loss prompted James to make a petition for a modification of the NBA's draft eligibility rules, which required prospective players to submit at least a high school diploma. He was then attempting to enter the 2002 NBA draft, but was unsuccessful.

James spent most of his senior year traveling around the country with the Fighting Irish. They played against nationally ranked teams including the Oak Hill Academy. This game was televised on ESPN2. Capitalizing on James' growing popularity, the Time Warner Cable offered a pay-per-view of St. Vincent-St. Mary's games to their subscribers for the entire season.

He achieved averages of 31.6 points, 5.6 assists, 9.6 rebounds, and 3.4 steals per game in his senior year. For the third consecutive year, James was selected for the USA Today's All-USA First Team and was named Ohio Mr. Basketball. For the second time, he earned the Gatorade National Player of the Year award.

James lost his NCAA eligibility when he participated in the Jordan Capital Classic, the McDonald's All-American Game, and the EA Sports Roundball. At the time, he was planning on entering the 2003 NBA draft.

His senior year was also a year of controversies for James. When he celebrated his 18th birthday, his mother secured a loan to get him a Hummer H2. She utilized James' future earning capacity as an NBA superstar. This violated the Ohio High School Athletic Association (OHSAA) bylaws, citing that amateurs cannot accept gifts worth more than $100 as a reward for their athletic performance.

An investigation was conducted by the association. In the end, he was cleared because the gift came from a family member and not from an outside source.

Afterward, James posed for pictures for an urban clothing store and accepted two throwback jerseys which were valued at $845. He officially violated the rules of the OHSAA. His high school sports eligibility was stripped. James made an appeal, resulting in a two-game suspension only.

The team also needed to forfeit one game, becoming their only loss during the season. When James returned to the court after his suspension, he recorded a career-high of 52 points. He led St. Vincent–St. Mary to winning the Division II title for the third time in the span of four years.

Football

Aside from basketball, James was also an exceptional football player. He was the St. Vincent-St. Mary's football team's wide receiver during his underclassman year. He was recruited by Notre Dame and other Division I programs.

At the end of his sophomore year, James earned the First Team All-State award. During his junior year, he led the Fighting Irish to win the state semifinals.

Unfortunately, he couldn't play in his senior year because he sustained a wrist injury during an AAU basketball game. A lot of football critics, sports analysts, high school coaches, and football players believed that he could have achieved great things in the National Football League if he chose to pursue it.

Chapter 2: The Early NBA Career of LeBron James

LeBron entered the 2003 NBA draft where he was chosen by his hometown team, the Cleveland Cavaliers, with the first overall pick.

Rookie Season: 2003-2004

James impressed everyone in his first regular-season game by scoring 25 points during a match between the Cavaliers and the Sacramento Kings. This score became the most points achieved by a prep-to-pro basketball player during his debut performance. He quickly became a league superstar and a favorite.

He averaged 20.9 points, 5.9 assists, and 5.5 rebounds per game during his rookie season. At the end of the season, James received his first NBA award as NBA Rookie of the Year. He was the first Cavalier to earn the honor, and only the third rookie player in the NBA to ever record at least 20 points, 5 assists, and 5 rebounds per game. The Cavaliers concluded the season with a 35-47 record, not making it to the playoffs despite having an 18-game improvement compared to their previous year.

Rising to Superstardom: 2004-2008

2004-05

When the Cavaliers won the 2004-2005 Eastern Conference, James had his first All-Star Game selection. He was able to contribute 13 points, 6 assists, and 8 rebounds during the game. Everyone in the league noticed his improvement in the short span of time. Denver Nuggets coach George Karl told Sports Illustrated that he felt weird saying that a 20-year old was a great player, but James was indeed a great one.

In a game against the Toronto Raptors on March 20, James scored 56 points. It set a new record of single-game points for Cleveland. At the end of the season, he got his first All-NBA Team selection by averaging 27.2 points, 7.2 assists, 7.4 rebounds, and 2.2 steals in every game. However, the team's 42-40 record was not enough to make it to the playoffs.

2005-06

This was a breakout year in James' pro-basketball career. He led the Eastern team to victory in the 2006 All-Star Game with 29 points. LeBron was named the Most Valuable Player in the All-Star Game. He finished second to Steve Nash during the voting of the overall NBA Most Valuable Player Award. He averaged 31.4 points, 6.6 assists, and 7 rebounds per game. James was also able to lead the Cavaliers to the playoffs; their first appearance since 1998.

During his postseason debut, James recorded a triple-double against the Washington Wizards. James made a game-winning shot in Game 3, and then again in Game 5 of the series. The Cavaliers won over the Wizards, but were ousted during the second round by the Detroit Pistons.

2006-07

James' averages during 2006-07 declined. He only recorded 27.3 points, 6 assists, 6.7 rebounds, and 1.6 steals per game. Analysts speculated that the regression of James' performance in passing skills and shot selection was due to a lack of focus and effort. Despite it, the Cavaliers ended the season with 50 wins, making it to the playoffs as the second seed in the East Conference.

James scored 48 points, 7 assists, and 9 rebounds during Game 5 of the NBA Conference Finals. He contributed 29 points to the team's final score and made an incredible game-winning lay-up versus the Pistons. His stellar performance was described by the play-by-play announcer Marv Albert as "one of the most amazing moments in post-season history."

He and his teammates dominated the court during Game 6, and finally achieved their first Eastern Conference Championship title. The Cavaliers got the chance to play against the San Antonio Spurs in the NBA Finals. James averaged 22 points, 6.8 assists, and 7.0 rebounds per game with a 35.6 % shooting performance during the championship series. However, the Cavaliers were no match for the Spurs, and lost the series 4 games to 0.

2007-08

James was named the All-Star Game's Most Valuable Player (MVP) in February of this season after a 27-point, 9-assist, and 8-rebound performance.

He surpassed Brad Daugherty on March 21 as the Cavaliers' All-Time leading scorer in a match versus the Raptors. This year he received his first scoring title. While James' individual scoring performances continued to improve, Cleveland's performance dropped, and they finished with a record of 45-37 for the year.

During the playoffs' first round, the fourth-seed Cavaliers defeated the Wizards. In the next round of seven games, they were eliminated by the Boston Celtics. LeBron James scored 45 points during the decisive final game versus the eventual-champions, while his opponent Paul Pierce scored 41 points. The game was described by the Associated Press as a "shootout".

2008-09

James finished the 2008-09 season with a career-high 93 total blocks, including 23 chase-down blocks. He was named to the

NBA All-Defensive Team for the first time and earned second place in NBA Defensive Player of the Year Award.

He became the fourth post-merger player ever to lead their team in points, assists, rebounds, blocks, and steals during a single season. His stellar performance and the arrival of All-Star guard Mo Williams helped Cleveland achieve a franchise record of 66-16. LeBron averaged 28.4 points, 7.2 assists, 7.6 rebounds, 1.7 steals, and 1.2 blocks per game.

In the history of Cleveland Cavaliers, James was their first player to achieve the Most Valuable Player Award. His performance was described by John Hollinger from ESPN as "the best individual season in NBA history".

During the playoffs, the Cavaliers defeated the Atlanta Hawks, and the Pistons. This earned them a place in the Conference Finals against the Orlando Magic.

During the series, James recorded 49 points in Game 1, but his team still narrowly lost. He led the team to victory in Game 2 to tie the series at 1-1. However, they lost 3 of the next 4 games and were eliminated. He was criticized by the media for leaving the court without shaking his opponents' hands after the final game. They called the act unsportsmanlike. He averaged an impressive 38.5 points, 8 assists, and 8.3 rebounds during the series.

2009-10

James played as a temporary point guard in February when many of his teammates suffered injuries. James' role as the primary ball handler significantly improved his stats. He recorded an average of 29.7 points, 8.6 assists, 7.3 rebounds, 1 block, and 1.6 steals per game on 50 percent shooting performance, earning him another MVP Award.

During the opening round of the playoffs, the Cleveland Cavaliers defeated the Chicago Bulls, earning a matchup against the Celtics. In Game 5, James was only able to score 15 points with 20% shooting. His performance was heavily criticized by the media and sports analysts.

Ultimately, the Cavaliers were eliminated in Game 6, despite LeBron recording 27 points, 10 assists, and 19 rebounds.

Chapter 3: Seasons of Change

After a disappointing end to the previous season, James made a big decision in 2010. He chose to leave Cleveland and become a free agent. It was regarded as one of America's most controversial free agent decisions in sports history. ESPN aired a program called 'The Decision' where the announcement was made.

2010

On July 1, 2010, at 12:01 a.m. EDT, LeBron James' became a free agent. It was a moment that many teams had been waiting for. He was approached by the Clippers, Bulls, Nets, Knicks, Heat, and of course, his former team the Cleveland Cavaliers.

After weighing his options, James made an announcement on July 8 on the live ESPN program named 'The Decision' that he would be signing with the Miami Heat. The live telecast which was held in the Boys & Girls Club of Greenwich, Connecticut raised $2.5 million in donations for the charity. Another $3.5 million from advertising revenues was given to other charities.

It wasn't James alone who made an announcement to join the Miami Heat. A day prior to the special TV coverage, free agents Dwayne Wade and Chris Bosh decided to sign up with the same team. There were speculations that the three players had been planning to join forces for some time. Rumors arose that James believed that their combined skills would seal his dream of securing an NBA championship. It would also lessen the pressure on him to carry his team offensively.

Later on, the Miami Heat President Pat Riley admitted that he sold the idea of playing with Wade and Bosh to James. He thought that it was best to relieve James of the burden to always lead his team in scoring.

LeBron's decision to leave the Cavaliers drew a lot of extreme criticisms from sports executives, sports analysts, former and active players, and basketball fans even before his formal announcement was made.

When Cavaliers owner Dan Gilbert learned that James would not return to them, he published an open letter denouncing his actions. Cavaliers' fans were furious and vented their disappointments in various ways. Some fans went viral after recording videos of them burning his numbered jersey.

Even NBA superstars Magic Johnson and Michael Jordan denounced his collaboration with Wade and Bosh. They had similar views that James was not man enough to win the championship for a team by himself.

His 2010 decision made LeBron James one of the most disliked athletes in America for a period of time.

2010-2011: Season of Scrutiny

LeBron James officially joined the Heat on July 10, 2010. He was only the third reigning Most Valuable Player ever to join a new team.

The Heat welcomed him, Wade, and Bosh with a rock-themed party on the evening of his contract signing at the American Airlines Arena. They were touted as the new "big three" in the basketball world. In a speech, James made a fearless claim that it was time for the Heat dynasty, referring to their potential multiple championships.

The event was not well-received by disappointed fans of the Cavaliers, and some sports critics.

Throughout the whole season, James and his new team were treated like villains by the fans of opposing teams. The media capitalized on it and continued attacking him. The Heat got off to a slow start, holding a 9-8 record after the first 17 games of the 2010-11 season. James later recalled that the constant scrutiny and criticism drove him to play with anger.

The game between the Heat and Cavaliers in Cleveland in December was a much-awaited game. For the first time, James would play against his former teammates. Every time James touched the ball, fans of the Cavaliers booed him. It didn't affect his performance though, and James was able to score 38 points and lead the Heat to a comfortable victory.

Throughout the season, the Heat improved and ended as the second seed in the Eastern Conference. James recorded an average of 26.7 points, 7 assists, and 7.5 rebounds per game, on 51% shooting.

During the conference semifinals, James and the Heat would go up against the Celtics. In Game 5, James sealed the win when he scored the last 10 points of the game. When the buzzer sounded, he emotionally knelt down on the floor of the court. Later on, James told the media reporters that their victory was not just a team triumph, but also an extremely personal accomplishment.

Eventually, they advanced to the Conference Finals but lost the chance to make the championship series when the Dallas Mavericks defeated them in six games. James averaged just 3 points during the fourth quarters of this series. He received another bout of negative criticisms for not taking the Heat to victory. LeBron's scoring average in the finals was just 17.8 points per game, which was an 8.9-point drop.

2011-2013: Seasons of back-to-back victory

In a retrospective moment, James admitted that their loss to the Mavericks humbled him and at the same time motivated him to leave the villain role behind. This decision helped him regain his joyful spirit on the court.

James took another positive step to improve his post-season game performance by working with Hakeem Olajuwon. His skills in the post improved significantly, and he led the Heat to an early season franchise-best record of 18-6. When the season ended, LeBron was named the Most Valuable Player for the 3rd time. He averaged 27.1 points, 6.2 assists, 7.9 rebounds, and 1.9 steals per game on 53% shooting.

During the playoffs, the Heat lost a game to the Indiana Pacers when Chris Bosh suffered an abdominal injury. James showed his skills in Game 4 to even the series 2-2, recording 40 points, 9 assists, and 18 rebounds. The Heat compensated for the absence of Bosh by playing James as the power forward. This new role remained even when Bosh returned during the Conference Finals when they faced the Celtics.

The do or die game in Game 6 drove James to record 45 points and 15 rebounds, leading the Heat to triumph. His astounding performance that night was described as a "career-defining moment" by The New York Times. They won the final game and advanced to the Finals against the Oklahoma City Thunder. James would be facing his budding rival, Kevin Durant.

In Game 4 of the Championship Series, James made a three-pointer shot that won the game. During Game 5, he recorded a triple-double which led them to victory in the series against the Thunder. It was the Heat's second championship, and LeBron's first.

His exemplary performance of 28.6 points, 7.4 assists, and 10.2 rebounds per game during the series resulted in a unanimous vote to become the Bill Russel NBA Finals Most Valuable Player. ESPN called his full post-season performance of 30.3 points, 5.6 assists, and 9.7 rebounds per game as the modern NBA history's second best.

During the 2012-13 season, James recorded an average of 29.7 points and 7.8 assists in February games. He also set multiple records of shooting efficiency. During this stretch, the Heat recorded the third longest winning streak in NBA history by winning 27 games consecutively.

He concluded the year with another MVP award; his fourth. He was just one vote away from getting the honor of being the first ever NBA player to earn it unanimously. His final averages for the season were 26.8 points, 7.3 assists, 8 rebounds, and 1.7

steals on 56.5% shooting. Miami ended the season with a league and franchise-best record of 66-16.

During the Conference Finals, James scored a buzzer-beating lay-up to win against the Pacers during Game 1. However, the team was struggling to help him to score all throughout the series, just like what he experienced in his 'Cleveland years'. Luckily, the Heat was able to overcome the challenges and met the Spurs in the Finals.

The next series of games signified a repeat of his first experience in the Finals six years ago. Once again, James' performance became a target of criticisms during the start of the series, citing his poor shot selection and lack of aggressiveness. The Heat fell behind in the series 2 games to 3.

Then, LeBron bounced back in Game 6 to avoid elimination, leading the Heat to a comeback win. James recorded his second triple-double during the series and scored 16 points during the fourth quarter alone. He played with more fervor in Game 7, leading Miami to victory against San Antonio, and securing his second NBA Championship. James averaged 25.3 points, 7 assists, 10.9 rebounds, and 2.3 steals per game during the championship series.

2013-2014: LeBron James' Final Season with the Heat

On March 3, James dropped a franchise-record and career-high 61 points when the Heat played against the Charlotte Bobcats. It was also a year in which the Heat would use 20 different starting lineups because of a series of injuries. James was forced to play various positions throughout the year, instead of his regular spot at the Small Forward position. He finished the season with an average of 27.1 points, 6.4 assists, and 6.9 rebounds per game on 56.7% shooting.

In Game 4 of the playoffs, James tied his career post-season high score of 49 points versus the Brooklyn Nets. They defeated the Pacers in the next round, earning the team another trip to the Finals.

When the Finals came, James suffered leg cramps during the fourth quarter of Game 1, resulting in an early loss against the Spurs. He did well in Game 2, leading the Heat with 35 points on 64% shooting to gain a series-tying win. But their chances ended with San Antonio winning the next 3 games. James' performances in the Finals gave him an average of 28.2 points, 2.0 steals, and 7.8 rebounds per game for the series.

Chapter 4: Returning to the Cavaliers

James ended his contract with the Miami Heat on June 25, 2014. He became an official unrestricted free agent on July 1.

His decision on July 11 to return to his former team, the Cleveland Cavaliers, surprised everyone. He made the announcement through a first-person essay via Sports Illustrated. It was well-received by fans, critics, colleagues, and media alike.

On July 12, James formally signed the contract to rejoin the Cavaliers. The team had a rough time without him, compiling a four-seasons league-worst record of 97-215. The Cavaliers further strengthened the team with the acquisition of Minnesota Timberwolves' Kevin Love. With Kyrie Irving, Kevin Love, and LeBron James, the Cavaliers were ready to rumble!

2014-2015

James missed the first two weeks of January games due to a lower back strain and left knee pain. It was his career's longest stretch of missed games, resulting in him playing a career-low of 69 games for the season. He ended with an average of 25.3 points, 7.4 assists, and 6 rebounds per game.

The Cavaliers won versus the Hawks in the Conference Finals, securing them a spot in the Finals. The victory made LeBron the first ever player make to five consecutive Finals since the 1960s. James took over more offensive responsibilities against the Warriors when Love and Irving suffered injuries.

He led the Cavaliers to a 2-1 lead, but he couldn't keep the wins coming. The Golden State Warriors won the next 3 games to secure the Championship. James averaged 35.8 points, 8.8 assists, and 13.3 rebounds per game during the Championship series. He was considered as a serious contender for the Finals MVP Award.

2015-16

Once again, James received a barrage of criticisms during this season when he became involved in off-court controversies, including the firing of the Cavalier's coach David Blatt mid-season. The Cavaliers, however, ended the year with an impressive record of 57 wins. It was the best record ever recorded in the Eastern Conference.

The Cavaliers advanced easily through the playoffs with only two losses to once again face the Golden State Warriors in the Championship series.

At the start of the much-awaited series, Cleveland suffered two losses, falling behind the Warriors 3 games to 1. In Games 5 and 6, James returned with a vengeance and registered back-to-back performances of 41 points, forcing a game 7.

James recorded a triple-double in Game 7 and made several key plays such as 'The Block' on Andre Iguodala. Cleveland emerged triumphant and won their first NBA Championship after 52 years! They also became the first ever team in the history of the NBA to return from a 3-1 deficit in a Championship series to become victorious.

LeBron recorded a series average of 29.7 points, 8.9 assists, 11.3 rebounds, 2.6 steals, and 2.3 blocks per game. He was the third player in NBA Finals history to score a triple-double, and finished as the unanimous choice as the Most Valuable Player in the Finals.

2016-2017

The Cavaliers suffered a lot of losses and injuries during this season. In January, James criticized the Cleveland management publicly by saying that they constructed a team that is too heavy to lead. The counter criticisms that he received were harsh. However, the team ended the season as the second seed in the East. He averaged 8.6 rebounds, 26.4 points, 8.7 assists, and 4.1 turnovers per game for the season.

James scored 41 points, 12 assists, and 13 rebounds in Game 3 against the Pacers during the first round of the playoffs. He led Cleveland back to victory, overcoming a 25-point deficit at halftime.

During Game 5 versus the Celtics in the Conference Finals, he scored 35 points and surpassed NBA superstar Michael Jordan as the All-Time post-season scoring leader of the league. They won the game as well as the series, securing a place in the Finals against the Warriors. The two teams would be playing against each other for the third consecutive time.

James recorded an average of 33.6 points, 10 assists, and 12 rebounds per game during the Championship series. Unfortunately, his performance wasn't enough, and Cleveland lost the series 4-1.

2017-2018

Before the start of the season, Kyrie Irving requested a trade with the Celtics. The move necessitated a major overhaul of the Cleveland roster.

The Cavaliers started the season well, winning 18 out of 19 games in December. During this month, James scored 57 points, the second-highest total points in his career. This performance also tied a franchise record.

When January came, the Cavaliers' performance dropped, and they experienced a losing record. Luckily, LeBron was able to rally, and the Cavaliers finished the season strongly. On March 30, he set the record of playing 867 straight games with double-digit scoring performances. He finished the season with a career-high average of 9.2 assists, on top of his 27.5 points, and 8.6 rebounds per game.

James became unstoppable in the playoffs, guiding the Cavaliers to another rematch with the Warriors in the Finals. In Game 1, Cleveland lost in overtime, despite James scoring a playoff career-high 51 points. The losses continued, and ultimately, they were swept in the series, losing 4-0.

June 2018

James chose to once again become an unrestricted free agent on June 29, 2018. His management firm, Klutch Sports, made an announcement on July 1 that the NBA superstar would be signing a contract with the Los Angeles Lakers. On July 6, the final negotiations were wrapped up.

Rich Paul, James' agent, told Sports Illustrated that the move was simply LeBron James doing what he wanted to do. He also explained that James' decision to play with Miami in 2010 was about championships. James' move to return to Cleveland in 2014 was about a delivery of a promise. Luckily, this recent decision to move to the Lakers was accepted positively by almost everyone.

Chapter 5: The Legacy of LeBron James

LeBron James is a versatile player who can play all five positions. He started as the Cavaliers' small forward, then began to play at power forward. He learned to skillfully switch between being the shooting guard, point guard, and center. This ability was honed during the times his teammates were injured, and he was left to step up.

Erik Spoelstra, his former coach at Miami, called him a *1-through-5* because he could do it all.

This ability to play every position helped in setting career records and achievements. Lebron's athletic skill and versatile playing style is often compared to NBA Hall of Famers Oscar Robertson, Michael Jordan, and Magic Johnson.

He is a four-time MVP player, three-time NBA champion, two-time Olympic Gold Medalist, and an all-star superstar of the modern NBA.

National Team Career

2004

James was chosen to be a member of Team USA who competed at the 2004 Olympics in Athens, Greece. In the eight games that they played, James only averaged 14.6 minutes, with 5.8 points and 2.6 rebounds in every game. He was still new to professional basketball and spent most of his time sitting on the bench. The United States national team went home with only a bronze medal. It was the first time that the national team concluded the Olympic Games without the coveted Gold Medal since the team added active NBA players to the lineup.

James told the press that he was treated unjustly and was not given ample opportunity to play in the Olympic Games. His limited playing time was a real "low light". His sour attitude was regarded by columnists Peter Vecsey and Adrian Wojnarowski as distasteful and disrespectful.

2006

James played a major role as co-captain for Team USA during the 2006 FIBA World Championship that was held in Japan. He recorded an average of 13.9 points, 4.1 assists, and 4.8 rebounds per game. The national team ended the tournament with an 8-1 performance record, bringing home another bronze medal.

The tournament was once again marred by controversy when teammate Bruce Bowen confronted James about how he treated the staff members.

2007

James had an outstanding performance during the FIBA Americas Championship, where he averaged 18.1 points, 4.7 assists, and 3.6 rebounds per game. During the championship game versus Argentina, he recorded 31 points which was the highest score ever made by an American player. They won the tournament with a 10-0 record, returning with a gold medal and a championship title. Team USA automatically qualified for the 2008 Olympics held in Beijing, China.

In an interview, James said that their improved play was due to a more positive attitude of the whole team.

2008

Before recruiting James to the 2008 Olympics team, he was given an ultimatum by Team USA coach Mike Krzyzewski and managing director Jerry Colangelo to improve his attitude.

James promised them he would do so, and played again for Team USA. The national team was undefeated during the Games and returned home with the Gold Medal. He recorded 14 points, 3 assists, and 6 rebounds during the final game against Spain.

2012

James opted not to join the team during the FIBA World Championship in 2010. He waited until 2012 to play again with Team USA during the 2012 Olympics in London, England.

He and Kobe Bryant led the national team. During that time, Bryant was already 34 and planning to step back. James facilitated the defensive sets or the offenses from the perimeter and the post, providing scoring when necessary.

James recorded a triple-double with 11 points, 12 assists, and 14 rebounds in a game versus Australia, which was the first triple-double in the history of US Olympics basketball.

They played against Spain in the final game, and emerged victories to win their second consecutive Gold Medal.

Team USA Coach Mike Krzyzewski was quoted saying that James *"was a great leader and the best player in the NBA"*.

This year proved to be one of the best years for James. He won the NBA MVP Award, NBA Finals MVP Award, NBA Championship, and an Olympic Gold Medal all in the same year. He joined Michael Jordan as the only players to ever achieve these feats.

LeBron James in the Offensive

When James started his career in Cleveland, he was used as the on-ball point forward. He displayed perimeter-oriented shooting tendencies before establishing himself as one of the best finishers and slashers.

At age 18, James led the Cavaliers in scoring. He was named Rookie of the Year.

He was the epitome of quickness, agility, and speed. This often caused matchup issues for opponents because James could easily overpower the smaller defenders and blow by the bigger ones.

During this period, he was often criticized for not being a good jump-shooter. His opponents exploited his weaknesses in the half court by giving him space which forced James to settle for long shots. This tactic was constantly used in the 2007 Finals by Coach Greg Popovich of Spurs to weaken James' performance, resulting in only a 36% shooting accuracy.

When James played with Miami, coach Spoelstra transferred him to a more conventional role. LeBron began spending more time in the post, improving his shot selection and shooting ability.

Upon his return to Cleveland, James began experiencing several age-related declines in productivity. This resulted in the lowest scoring averages of his career. His shooting ability suffered, and he was briefly ranked in the NBA as the worst high-volume outside shooter. However, despite injury challenges, James remained a tenacious offensive player with an amazing ability to beat defenses with his varied attacking speed, strength, and body control.

One of his best skills is his ability as a play-maker. James utilizes his vision, size, and attention he receives from the opponents' defense to his advantage. He has been ranked by sports analysts as one of the greatest passers in the history of NBA.

LeBron James in the Defensive

James was not a particularly good defensive player when he began his NBA career. Gradually, he overcame this weakness through constant and consistent practice.

By 2009, James had mastered the chase-down block. Miami used him, Dwyane Wade, and Shane Battier to form an ultra-aggressive defense.

Today, LeBron is regarded as one of the league's best defensive players, with one of his most memorable plays being 'The Block' that he performed against the Golden State Warriors' Andre Iguodala in the 2015-16 Finals series!

Chapter 6: Life Off the Court

Personal Life

LeBron James is more than just a basketball superstar. He has huge influence off of the court, and stories from his personal life are regularly deemed newsworthy. This chapter will dive in to LeBron's personal life so you can get a better understanding of what the man is like outside of basketball!

Single life

During a split-up with current wife Savanna, James dated Adrienne Bailon. The American songwriter, singer, dancer, television personality, and actress, was the founder and lead singer of 3LW and The Cheetah Girls group. The couple became engaged on December 23, 2003. They broke off the engagement in February 2004 and ended their 9-month relationship. They never made an official explanation about their separation.

Marriage

On September 14, 2013, James tied the knot with Savanna in San Diego, California. The lavish wedding featured Beyonce and Jay-Z who performed "Crazy in Love." The three-day wedding festivities included a lot of celebrities, fellow NBA players, and close family friends.

James and Savanna were high school sweethearts. They both grew up in Akron, Ohio but attended different high schools. While James was making a name as a sports prodigy in football and basketball, Savanna was a softball player and a cheerleader.

They first met at a football game. It didn't take LeBron long to ask Savanna to watch him play. Savanna accepted and was surprised to learn that James was a great basketball player.

Their first date was at Outback Steakhouse. Savana recalled that she left the leftovers in James' car, who immediately returned to give them to her. In one interview, she joked that perhaps it was his excuse to come and see her again.

Savanna said that she never imagined that her sweetheart would become one of the kings of the NBA. She only believed that this tall guy on campus would become a hometown sports hero. James became much more than she expected, and she was happy for him.

During their senior years, Savanna fell pregnant with their eldest child. She was scared during that time, but James told her that he would be there all throughout, supporting her while he would keep doing what he was doing. The pregnancy would not slow him or them down, according to James. James was there to take her to the senior prom despite his busy schedule.

On the eve of December 31, 2011, James proposed to her at the Shelborne Sought Beach Hotel in Miami. It was also his 27th birthday. His colleague and friend, Dwyane Wade, was the one holding the $300,000 engagement ring for him during the proposal.

After the wedding, James posted this message to his Instagram account- *"So happy to call you Mrs. Savannah James."*

At present, the couple has three children, named Bryce Maximus James, Zhuri James, and LeBron James Jr.

The following year after their wedding, James surprised his wife on her 30th birthday with a Miami Vice-themed party. It was one of Savanna's favorite TV shows. She was overwhelmed with happiness which doubled up when James gifted her with a Ferrari Testarossa, the car that was used in the show.

Public Life

Career

James is called the "face of the NBA" by a lot of people, including his co-players. He fights for what is right and beneficial for the players. One of his significant actions was asking Commissioner Adam Silver to increase the All-Star break duration in 2014. On February 13, 2015, he was elected as the National Basketball Players Association (NBPA) vice president.

His professional career has been represented by Klutch Sports agent Rich Paul since 2012. Before that, James' agent was Aaron Goodwin, then followed by Leon Rose in 2005. In 2007, Rose joined Creative Artists Agency (CAA). He worked with fellow agent Henry Thomas, who was representing Chris Bosh and Dwayne Wade in persuading James to sign with the Miami Heat back in 2010.

After James left CAA, he established LRMR, an agent & sports-marketing firm together with friends Paul, Maverick Carter, and Randy Mims. LRMR stands for Lebron, Paul, Maverick, and Randy. The company handled his marketing, including the highly-criticized *The Decision*.

James is obviously a wise businessman. Throughout his basketball career he has made many smart decisions. He has taken a unique approach to signing his NBA contracts, by opting for shorter-term deals to retain flexibility and optimize his earning potential. In 2006, he negotiated a 3-year contract extension worth $60 million with the Cavaliers, instead of 4 years.

James' unrestricted free agent status allowed him to accept a bigger contract in the 2010 season. He signed with the Heat after the team got Bosh and Wade.

When James returned to the Cleveland Cavaliers, he chose to re-sign a new contract every season to take advantage of the NBA's rising salary cap. His 3-year deal with the Cavaliers in 2016 made him the highest-paid player.

Media Influencer

James has been a perennial rank holder of Forbes' list of Most Influential Athletes. In 2017, Time listed him as one of the 100 World's Most Influential People.

When he started his career at Cleveland, Sherwin-Williams displayed Nike-produced banners of James at its stores across the world. His moves are always closely watched and reported by the press.

LeBron has had a love-hate relationship with fans and critics. When James made his controversial decision to become a free agent in 2010, he became one of the most disliked athletes in the United States of America. In 2013, ESPN described him as the most popular NBA player, regaining his positive public image. The following year, James was named by the Harris Poll as America's most popular male athlete. In terms of jersey sales, he has led the league six times.

Advertisements

Capitalizing on his popularity and influence, many companies have wanted James to endorse their products. He has endorsed Coca-Cola, Nike, McDonalds, Audemars Piguet, Beats by Dre, State Farm, and Dunkin' Brands.

Three giant shoe companies Nike, Adidas, and Reebok had a bidding-war to sign right after he finished high school. James chose Nike and signed an approximately $90-million contract. His Nike signature shoes have earned massive profits for the company.

When he let Fenway Sports Group become his rights' sole global marketer in 2011, James gained a minority stake in Liverpool, one of England's premier football teams. This decision further increased his net worth, making him one of the highest-paid athletes in the world.

In 2013, James earned a total of $56.5 million. This made him the world's highest-paid basketball player, outranking Kobe Bryant.

During Apple's acquisition of Beats Electronics in 2014, James' small stake when he made a deal to promote their headphones during its inception stage gave him more than $30-million in profit.

In 2015, James was listed as the sixth highest earning athlete. In 2016, he ranked third after Cristiano Ronaldo and Lionel Messi. In one interview, James said he dreamed of one day having his own team in the NBA.

Movies and Entertainment

With a knack for comedy, James tried his luck at hosting. During the ESPY Awards in 2007, he was the co-host of Jimmy Kimmel. James also hosted the premiere of the 33rd season of *Saturday Night Live*.

In 2009, James and Maverick Carter founded SpringHill Entertainment and produced the Lions Gates documentary film More Than a Game, a chronicle of his high school life. Other series that they produced were Disney XD sports documentary show *Becoming*, the animated web series *The Lebrons*, Startz sitcom *Survivor's Remorse*, and *The Wall* game show of the NBC.

James also tried acting and appeared in a cameo role in *Entourage*, an HBO series. He portrayed himself in *Trainwreck*, a Judd Apatow film in 2015. His acting performance received positive reviews.

To enhance the capacity to produce athlete-created content shows to fans all over the world, his digital video company Uninterrupted raised a staggering $15.8 million from Turner Sports and Warner Bros. Entertainment.

In 2016, James and business partner Maverick Carter produced a reality show series called *Cleveland Hustles*. The unscripted shows that were aired on CNBC featured 4 Northern Ohio aspiring entrepreneurs whose ventures they financed in exchange for helping to revitalize the Cleveland neighborhood.

They also joined Future the Prince and rapper Drake to produce the Carter Effect, a 60-minute Vince Carter documentary during the 2017 Toronto International Film Festival.

During the early part of 2018, his production company made an announcement that they would be producing a new film based on the House Party series, with James to make a cameo role.

James would also star in Space Jam 2, the sequel of Michael Jordan and Looney Tunes characters hit movie. In an interview, he told the *Hollywood Reporter* that he wanted the kids to understand that empowerment comes from feeling that they are strong and capable and by not giving up on their dreams. The long-awaited project, which will be directed by Terence Nance and produced by Ryan Coogler, will commence filming during the 2019 NBA off-season.

In February, Fox News journalist Laura Ingraham voiced her negative opinion regarding James' political agenda and told him to *"Shut up and dribble"*. In response, James hosted a documentary series that looked into athletes' changing role amidst the present cultural and political environment. The show was named "Shut Up and Dribble" and aired on Showtime.

James was the first black man to appear on the cover of Vogue, posing with Gisele Bündchen in the March 2008 issue. He became the third man overall after George Clooney and Richard Gere to pose for the prestigious magazine.

Charity Work

James is also a notable philanthropist. In 2004, he and his mother founded the LeBron James Family Foundation to provide assistance to single parents and children in need. One of the programs of the foundation is to build playgrounds in poor neighborhoods. To raise money to fund its various programs, the foundation holds a yearly bike-a-thon event.

The foundation has donated $41 million to fund the scholarship of poor but deserving students of the University of Akron. In 2015, James made a public announcement that he had partnered with the university with the aim of educating 2,300 children at the college by 2021. The program is already rolling and has financed more than a thousand kids already.

He actively supports the Boys & Girls Clubs of America, Children's Defense Fund, and After-School All-Star, among other non-profit organizations.

In 2016, James supported the Muhammad Ali exhibit by donating $2.5 million to the Smithsonian National Museum of African-American History and Culture.

In 2017, he received the NBA's J. Walter Kennedy Citizenship Award for his "outstanding service and dedication to the community." During the same year, his "I Promise School" project was finally approved by the Akron School Board. It is a public elementary school for about 1,000 at-risk children who are in grades 1-8. It was formally opened on July 30, 2018.

James was quoted saying that this project was his most important professional life achievement.

Political Activism

James is not afraid to express his own views and opinions on political affairs. He is known for taking strong stances on controversial public issues. He once said that he felt a sense of obligation to use his status to effect a significant change.

After a 2007 Los Angeles racist incident, James said that belonging to the black race is difficult and that African Americans have a long way to go until they feel equal in America.

In 2012, James was vocal in his support for Trayvon Martin, following the teen's death. He tweeted – *"The fatal shooting of 17-year-old Trayvon Martin "hit a switch for me. From that point on, I knew that my voice and my platform had to be used for more than just sports."*

James told Don Lemon of CNN that Martin's death became his catalyst to find his own voice. He realized that it was important for him to use his voice and platform not just for sports but also for social issues.

During the interview, Lemon and James discussed some policies of President Donald Trump. James was outspoken in his disagreement and openly criticized the President. According to him, the highest office in the land should be utilized for more relevant matters and not just economic gains for Trump's sponsors and family.

He and his teammates in Miami Heat took another step to seek justice for Martin. James tweeted an iconic photo showing them wearing hooded sweatshirts of the Miami Heat, unified and rallying against injustice. He used the hashtags #WeWantJustice, #WeAreTrayvonMartin, #Hoodies, and #Stereotyped.

He has also served as a strong voice on the death of Eric Garner, War in Darfur, and the racist comments of former NBA owner Donald Sterling in 2014.

In the aftermath of Charlottesville, Virginia 2017 Unite the Right rally, James displayed his dislike of Trump's slogan "Make America Great Again." He was quoted saying *"Is this the direction our country is heading?"* He also said that the youth deserve better. When Trump retracted the White House invitation to another basketball superstar Stephen Curry, James was the first one to react and called the President a "bum".

During an interview with CNN in 2018, James accused Trump of attempting to divide America with sports. He was quoted saying that *"sports have never been something to divide people, it brings them together."* He also said that he would sit across from Barack Obama, but never with Trump.

Trump responded by saying the dumbest man on TV was Don Lemon, because he portrayed LeBron James to look smart, and it was not easy to do. Trump's tweet didn't receive any positive response from many players. Former NBA Champion Michael Jordan supported James and disavowed the President's statement.

A strong supporter of Obama, James donated $20,000 in June 2008 to a committee to vote for the Democratic Presidential nominee. He also gathered around 20,000 people to view the 30-minute television advertisement of Obama entitled American Stories, American Solutions on a large screen at the Quicken Loans Arena. The showing was followed by a free Jay-Z concert.

In November 2016, James endorsed Democratic Presidential candidate Hillary Clinton.

Social Media Influencer

James uses social media to express his opinions on relevant socio-cultural-political issues. At the time of writing, he has 22.7 million followers on Facebook, 41.8 million Twitter followers, and 38.7 million followers on Instagram.

Chapter 7: Records & Achievements

It cannot be denied that James was one of the most celebrated basketball prospects during his high school years. He was young, agile, and skillful.

Immediately after an impressive performance during his first season in the NBA, James was named Rookie of the Year.

He has played in the Finals 9 times, winning three championships. He has won the Finals Most Valuable Player three times, which is the second most an NBA player has ever won.

From 2009-2014, James was named every season as an All-Defensive player. However, he has never once won the Defensive Player of the Year Award. He finished in the second place twice.

James is highly-regarded as one of the greatest NBA players of all-time by the media.

- In February 2016, Sports Illustrated ranked him 5th.
- In March 2016, he was ranked 5th by ESPN.
- In February 2017, CBS Sports ranked him as 2nd.
- In December 2017, Fox Sports placed him 2nd.
- In February 2018, he was ranked 2nd by Slam Magazine.

His magnificent skills and strength on the court are often compared to Michael Jordan. One significant study was conducted by Bill Simmons during February 2018. He spent a whole week comparing the two superstars on his website, The Ringer, concluding at the end that Jordan was still way ahead of James.

ESPN's sportswriter Brian Windhorst who spent a lot of time covering James' basketball career was quoted saying- *"No one has ever had as much as he had to live up to, and delivered every last drop."*

Career Stats and Points

As of January 2018, he became the seventh player in the NBA to accumulate 30,000 career points, surpassing Kobe Bryant as the youngest player to achieve this feat. It placed him closer to Kareem Abdul-Jabbar's 38,387 points.

His averages per game include:

- 27 points
- 1.2 offensive rebounds
- 6.1 defensive rebounds
- 1.6 steals
- 7.2 assists
- 3.5 turnovers
- 0.8 blocks
- 0.344 3-point field goal percentage
- 0.739 free-throw percentage
- 0.504 field-goal percentage

Summary of LeBron James' Awards and Honors

High School

- 2003 National Champion
- 2003 Naismith Prep Player of the Year
- 2003 EA Sports Roundball Classic MVP
- 2003 McDonald's National Player of the Year
- 2003 McDonald's All-American Game 2003
- 2003 McDonald's High School All-American
- 2003 Most Valuable Player of Jordan Capital Classic
- 3 times Champion in OHSAA (2000, 2001, 2003)

- 3 times All-USA First Team of USA Today (2001, 2002, 2003)
- 3 times Ohio Mr. Basketball (2001, 2002, 2003)
- 2 times PARADE High School Player of the Year (2002, 2003)
- 2 times High School Player of the Year of USA Today (2002, 2003)
- 2 times National Player of the Year of Gatorade (2002, 2003)
- Hall of Famer in St. Vincent-St. Mary (Class of 2011)
- Number 23 retired by St. Vincent-St. Mary
- St. Vincent-St. Mary basketball home court was renamed to The LeBron James Arena.

NBA Career

- 4 times Most Valuable Player of NBA (2009, 2010, 2012, 2013)
- 3 times Most Valuable Player of NBA Finals (2012, 2013, 2016)
- 3 times Most Valuable Player of NBA All-Star Game (2006, 2008, 2018)
- 3 times NBA Champion (2012, 2013, 2016)
- 14 times All-NBA Star (2005 to 2018)
- 14 times All-NBA selection
- 12 times First Team (2006, 2008 to 2018)
- 2 times Second Team (2005, 2007)
- 6 times NBA All-Defensive selection
- 5 times First Team (2009 to 2013)
- 1 time Second Team (2014)
- 3 times minutes- leader in the NBA (2007, 2017, 2018)
- 2008 NBA Scoring Champion
- 2004 Rookie of the Year
- 2004 All-Rookie First Team
- 2017 J. Walter Kennedy Citizenship Awardee

National Team

- 2 times Olympic Gold Medalist (2008, 2012)
- 2012 Male Athlete of the Year of USA Basketball
- 2007 FIBA Americas Championship Gold Medal winner
- 2006 FIBA World Championship Bronze Medal winner
- 2004 Olympic Bronze Medal winner
- Commemorative banner in the American Airlines Arena in Miami (for his Gold Medal award as Miami Heat team member)

Other Achievements

- 3 times Cleveland Sports Awardee as Professional Athlete of the Year (2009, 2016, 2017)
- 2 times Sportsperson of the Year awardee of Sports Illustrated (2012, 2016)
- 2 times AP Athlete of the Year awardee (2013, 2016)
- 2 times Hickok Belt Winner (2012, 2013)
- 19 times ESPY Award winner in different categories (4 as part of the team and 15 as individual awards)
- 2004 Sporting News Rookie of the Year
- 2006 Sporting News NBA MVP
- 2012 Sporting News Athlete of the Year
- 2011-12 EFL Cup Champion (being part-owner of the Liverpool F.C.)
- 2017 NAACP Image Awards- Jackie Robinson Award
- Sports Illustrated NBA All-Decade First Team (the 2000s)
- Honorary football and basketball lockers at Ohio State facilities
- Akron's South Main Street was renamed King James Way
- Six-story commemorative banner in Akron
- Three-story mural to honor his contract signing with the Lakers in Venice, California

Movies and Television Shows

Movies

- 2008 – More Than a Game
- 2009 – Square Roots: The Story of Sponge Bob Square Pants
- 2015 – Trainwreck
- 2018 – Smallfoot (Gwangi voice)

Television

- 2009 – Entourage (Give a Little Bit Episode)
- 2009- My Wife and Kids (Outbreak Monkey Episode)
- 2009- SpongeBob's Truth or Square
- 2011 – 2014 – The LeBrons
- 2015 – Survivor's Remorse (Guts Episode)
- 2016 – Teen Titans Go! (The Cruel Giggling Ghoul episode)
- 2018 – The Shop

Chapter 8: The Journey Continues

During the Finals against the Golden State Warriors, James said that his family, especially his kids would be a huge part of his next move in his career.

His decisions in 2010 and 2014 were huge news. When his deal with Miami Heat was announced in 2010, 13-million viewers tuned in to The Decision via ESPN. James said that the first time he left Cleveland was because he felt that he didn't possess the level of talent for the competition.

James had just completed his eighth-straight NBA Finals series, leading in minutes played. He averaged 27.5 points, a career-high of 9.1 assists, and 8.6 rebounds per game.

According to one witness who was there when James talked to a confidant, the basketball superstar said that if he would leave Cleveland again, his decision would also be fulfilling a childhood dream.

Weighing the Options

Prior to his decision, everyone was anticipating his move because he held the key to the power balance in the NBA. He had the player option to command $35.6 million for a 3-year contract in 2018-19 season.

At this point in his career and after playing for 15 years in the NBA, James already knew which franchises could offer worthy deals. However, regardless of where he signed, King James would remain one of the highest-paid players based on his annual endorsement income of more than $50-million.

The Cavaliers could offer him a 5-year deal worth $205 million if James chose to stay.

Many were betting that James was bound for the Los Angeles Lakers. The Lakers had the most salary cap at $62-million, enough to sign both him and Paul George who was also a free agent.

The BIG Decision 2018

The waiting was finally over. LeBron James chose to move to the next chapter of his colorful basketball career when he signed with the Lakers on July 1, 2018. A simple, old-school press release confirmed the four-year, $154 million deal with the legendary franchise.

First Media Day

On September 24, 2018, James spoke in front of the press wearing his number 23 purple-and-gold Lakers uniform. It was his first official public appearance as a member of the Los Angeles Lakers.

The excited media was waiting for James to expound his reasons for joining the Lakers and leaving Cleveland for the second time, but the superstar was tight-lipped.

For 15 minutes, he casually faced and answered the questions from the reporters after paying homage to the team's history, all-time great players, and 16 NBA championships. He also talked about adhering to the team's process. Magic Johnson was on a nearby balcony, listening to James.

When he was asked if he would be mixing sports with business in Los Angeles, James responded by saying – *"I play ball. I am a basketball player."* He reiterated that that's what he lived by.

James also told the press that nothing could pressure him anymore and his only aim was to get better every day, saying

"What I can bring to the table is being committed to having excellence every single day."

Win-Win Affair

James' production company Springhill Entertainment is based in L.A. His family has a pair of off-season homes in the area. For people close to him, the decision to leave the Cavaliers was a good move. For James it was a much better experience this time around because there were no angry outbursts from the fans of the Cavaliers.

It was also a great accomplishment for the management team of Lakers comprised of Magic Johnson, Jeanie Buss, and Rob Pelinka whose mission was to sign a legend worthy of the Lakers' gold and purple jersey and a basketball hero worthy of Hollywood.

The King has arrived

After the official announcement that King James would sign the deal with the Lakers, the Staples Center Team L.A. shop sold all their No. 23 jerseys in less than 24 hours.

The web portal of the Lakers team store buzzed with orders, too. Replicas of his new uniform were sold for $75 while James' T-Shirts were priced at $35.

Conclusion

Thanks again for taking the time to read this book!

You should now have a good understanding of the incredible life and career of LeBron James!

If you enjoyed this book, please take the time to leave me a review on Amazon. I appreciate your honest feedback, and it really helps me to continue producing high quality books.

www.ingramcontent.com/pod-product-compliance
Lightning Source LLC
Chambersburg PA
CBHW061102050726
47592CB00004B/1793